# SEE IT, COOK IT!

# SEE IT, COOK IT!

EASY-TO-DO, FOOL-PROOF RECIPES FOR THE WOULD-BE GOURMET

PHOTOGRAPHY BY
OLIVER BRACHAT

→ Illustrated by
Christiane Weismüller

Skyhorse Publishing

# table of contents

------------------------------------------------

## DESSERTS

more!

# APPETIZERS

½ cup (125 g) crème fraîche

1½ tbsp (30 g) mustard
2 tsp wine vinegar
¼ cup + 1 tbsp (75 ml) olive oil

2 cloves garlic

½ bunch parsley
½ bunch chives
6 tomatoes

1 AVOCADO

1 cucumber

**3 green onions**

VARIOUS SALAD GREENS,
I.E., ENDIVE, ARUGULA,
ICEBERG LETTUCE

10 radishes
3 carrots

*1 LARGE RED ONION*

salt + pepper

# salad in a jar

Wash the salad greens and dry them well. Tear them into bite size pieces. Wash the cucumber and tomatoes and cut them into slices. Peel the onion and slice into thin rings. Take the skin off the avocado, remove the seed, and *carefully* dice. Wash the radishes and cut them into slices. Wash the green onions and cut them into fine rings. Peel the carrots and cut them into sticks. Wash the herbs, pat them dry, and chop them finely. Place everything into either a canning or a mason jar, alternating vegetables by layer.

For the dressing, mix the crème fraîche, mustard, and vinegar together. Peel the garlic, chop it finely, and add it to the mixture. Stir in the olive oil drop by drop, using a whisk, so that a homogeneous mass takes shape. Season with salt and pepper. Pour the dressing into another jar, and then, ideally, bring everything with you on a picnic.

2 cups (200 g) fresh or frozen cranberries

12 midsize frozen shrimp without heads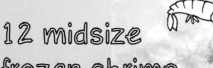

1 large onion

juice from 1 lime

2 TBSP

SUN-FLOWER OIL

4 SLICES TOASTED BREAD

1 red chili pepper

SALT PEPPER

2 pinches cumin

3 tbsp granulated brown sugar

ginger to taste

# SPICY SHRIMP TOAST

Clean the shrimp and pat them dry.
Peel the ginger and cut it into
small pieces. Puree both of
them finely and season
with salt and
pepper. Clean the
chili pepper and
chop it up. Add
crushed cumin and
half of the lime
juice to the shrimp
mixture. Mix well and spread
smoothly onto
the slices of toast up
until the edges. Cut
in half diagonally.

Wash the cranberries
and cut them in half.
Peel the onion and chop it
up finely. Heat up 1 tbsp oil in a
pot, place the onions and sugar in it, and
let them caramelize a little bit. Add the cranberries and let cook, covered, for
15 minutes. Monitor the pan to ensure that the chutney does not burn. Then, add
the rest of the lime juice and season to taste with salt and pepper.

Heat up 1 tbsp oil in a pan. Cook the shrimp toasts, first on the coated side,
and then on the backside, for two minutes each. Serve with the chutney.

SERVES
4

**10** *different colored carrots* (total weight approx. 2¼ lbs [1 kg])

**3** SPRIGS OF ROSEMARY

**10 TBSP OLIVE OIL**

PEPPER    SALT

1⅓ lbs (600 g) *waxy potatoes*

4 PARSLEY ROOTS

12

# Rosemary Roasted Vegetables

Wash and peel the vegetables. Cook the potatoes in a generous amount of salted water for 10 minutes. Drain and place in a baking pan.

Cut the parsley roots and carrots into approx. 2-in (5-cm) long sticks. Put into the pan with the potatoes. Pour in olive oil and toss well.

Preheat the oven to 390°F (200°C), or 355°F (180°C) for a convection oven. Place the pan in the oven and let the vegetables stew for about 45 minutes. Every once in a while, stir carefully, using a spoon. After about 20 minutes, add the sprigs of rosemary. As soon as the vegetables are ready, remove from the oven and season heartily with salt and pepper.

serves 4

1 bunch chives

1 small celeriac

1 ONION, HALVED + ROASTED

3 Carrots

2 Marrowbones

26 oz (750 g) beef

1 leek

1 PACKAGE VERMICELLI

juniper berries
5

peppercorns
8

CLOVES
5

sea salt

5-6 bay leaves

14

Heat up 13 cups of water in a big pot. Let the meat as well as the marrowbones simmer for about an hour.

Wash and chop ⅔ of the vegetables. Add halved onions and spices to the meat. Salt everything lightly and let simmer for another hour.

# Beef Soup

Take the pot off the stove and let it cool. Take the meat out, remove the vegetables and spices, and strain the broth. Wash the leftover vegetables. Peel the celeriac and carrots, dice them, and cut the leeks into rings. Cook the noodles in hot water, drain them, and rinse with cold water. Blanch the vegetables, and pull the meat into bite-sized pieces.

To serve, heat up the broth, add meat and vegetables, and season with salt. Spread noodles on a plate and fill it up with the hot soup. Garnish with chopped chives.

14 oz (400 g)
lamb's lettuce

150 g
bacon

2 tbsp
butter

3 slices
coarse brown
bread with
crust

1 garlic
clove

SALT

PEPPERCORNS

2 tbsp
white wine
vinegar

2 OZ
(60G)
POTATOES

1 cup + 1 tbsp
(250 ml)
vegetable
broth

3 tbsp + 1 tsp
(50 ml) cream

4 tbsp
sun-
flower
oil

16

# lamb's lettuce salad with potato dressing

Peel the potatoes and the garlic clove, cut them into small pieces, and put them in a pot with vegetable broth. Let it cook for 20 minutes. Add cream and let it cool. Next, add oil and vinegar, and puree using a blender. If the dressing is still a bit too thick, add a little vegetable broth. Season with salt and pepper.

Dice the bacon and fry it in a pan until crisp. Let it dry on paper towels. Place butter in the pan with the leftover fat. As soon as the butter begins to get frothy, throw in bread, which has been diced into fairly large pieces, and fry until crispy. Wash the salad and arrange it on a plate, drizzle with a little bit of dressing, and garnish with bacon and croutons.

SERVES 4

Tip: You can also mix the lamb's lettuce with other types of lettuce, for example with rucola, chicory, or iceberg lettuce.

17

(500 ml) vegetable broth

3 GARLIC CLOVES

1 can coconut milk

1 tsp butter

½ chili pepper

5 tsp (25 g) ginger

TWO APPLES

1 PINCH GROUND CINNAMON

1 onion

1 tsp granulat[ed] brown su[gar]

10-12 halves of walnut seeds

1 SMALL HOKKAIDO PUMPKIN

1 TSP POWDERED SUGAR

and additionally:
- salt
- pumpkin seed oil for garnishing

# PUMPKIN AND GINGER SOUP

## SERVES 4

Peel the pumpkin, cut it in half, remove the seeds, and dice. Wash the apples, core them, and cut them into small pieces. Peel the onions, and chop them into small pieces as well. Wash the chili pepper and slice it into rings. Put everything into a pot along with the vegetable broth and bring to a boil. Let simmer for approx. 30 minutes without a lid.

Add coconut milk, cinnamon and brown sugar. Bring to a boil again and add butter. Puree the soup with a blender. Season with salt. Chop the walnuts and roast them in an ungreased pan. Sprinkle the nuts with powdered sugar, and stir the two ingredients together. Pour the soup into little bowls and sprinkle with walnuts. Garnish with a few splashes of pumpkin seed oil.

19

1 lb (500 g)
waxy potatoes

1 TBSP
BUTTER

**2 zucchini
(12.4oz/350g)**

*freshly ground
black pepper*

1 TBSP CORNSTARCH

1 tbsp mild mustard
**2 tbsp honey**
2 tbsp crème fraîche

Salt

22

2 tbsp concentrated
butter

250 g smoked
salmon,
sliced thinly

1 TSP FINELY
CHOPPED
DILL

# Zucchini Rosti with Smoked Salmon

PREHEAT THE OVEN TO 360°F (180°C), OR 320°F (160°C) FOR A CONVECTION OVEN.

SERVES 4

Wash the potatoes, peel them, and grate them coarsely using a grater. Wash the zucchini and cut it into thin slices. Mix those two ingredients together with a pinch of salt and the cornstarch. Heat up the concentrated butter in a non-stick pan. Add the potato-zucchini mixture and flatten with a spatula.

Fry on medium heat for about 2 minutes or until the rosti is golden brown. Then, place everything, including the pan, into the oven and let it cook for about 15 minutes. Afterward, take it out again and flip the rosti using a spatula.

Fry the second side until golden brown as well, adding a few pats of butter around the corners. Season with salt and pepper. Mix the mustard with honey and crème fraîche, season with salt and pepper, and proceed to mix in the dill. Serve the rosti with salmon and the honey-mustard sauce.

¼ cup (50 g) cold butter

⅔ cup (150 ml) white wine

3 cups (700 ml) vegetable broth

2 sprigs rosemary

2 sprigs thyme

5 tbsp olive oil

2 shallots

2 garlic cloves

S P

Tip:
Other mushrooms can also be substituted, i.e. Caesar's mushroom, oyster mushrooms, or porcini

¼ cup (50 g) grated parmesan

21 oz (600 g) mixed mushrooms

1 ¼ cup (250 g) risotto

# mushroom risotto

Peel the shallots and garlic and dice finely.
Grate the Parmesan cheese finely. Heat up
2 tbsp olive oil in a large pot, and use it
to lightly sauté the shallots and garlic.
Add the rice and stir until glassy. Pour the
white wine over the top and let the mixture
boil down. Pour ¼ of the broth in and let
the rice cook, stirring frequently, until the
grains have almost completely absorbed the
liquid. Repeat this step three times, until the
broth has all been used. This takes about 20 min.

Preheat the oven to 430°F (220°C), or 390°F (200°C)
with a convection oven. Wash the mushrooms and cut
them into slices or quarters. Spread them out on a
baking pan, drizzle with the leftover olive oil,
and add the plucked rosemary needles and thyme
leaves. Allow the mushrooms to simmer in the oven
for about 15 minutes. Season with salt and pepper.

Season the risotto with salt and pepper as well.
Take the pot off the stove and mix in the
cold butter. For a creamy consistency,
mix in the grated Parmesan, and
serve with the mushrooms.

Serves 4

25

4 ¼ cups (¼ l) vegetable broth

½ ONION, FINELY DICED

**12**
Romano peppers

Peel from ½ organic lemon

2 GREEN ONIONS (60 G)

1 clove garlic (or more, to taste)

1 pinch pepper

½ CUP (80 G) FETA CHEESE

1 tsp salt

1 tsp ground Ceylon cinnamon

½ TSP CUMIN

4 tbsp olive oil

**3 SPRIGS THYME**

**1 lb (500 g) ground lamb**

# STUFFED ROMANO PEPPERS

Serves 4

Preheat the oven to 390°F (200°C), or for a convection oven 355°F (180°C). Clean the peppers, and, with a sharp knife, cut a ⅓-inch (1-cm) wide piece out of each. Remove the seeds. Grease a baking pan with 1 tbsp olive oil and place the peppers inside, next to each other.

Spoon in the ground lamb, peel the garlic, and chop up finely. Add diced onion, the lemon zest, the spices, and 1 tbsp olive oil to the meat and mix everything together. Dice the feta cheese into small pieces, clean the green onions, and slice into thin rings.

Mix both of them in with the meat mixture, and if desired, add further seasonings to taste.

Fill the peppers with the mixture, and then pour the vegetable broth over the top. Distribute the rest of the oil on top of the peppers and add the sprigs of thyme. Cook in the oven for approx. 30 minutes.

Salt

1 ¾ CUP (220 G) FLOUR

2 TBSP CANOLA OIL

½ CUP (125 ML) WATER

**2 apples**

PEPPER

3 oz (80 g)
goat cheese

1 TBSP
MILK

2 TBSP
OLIVE OIL

4 sprigs
rosemary,
needles
removed

9 oz (250 g)

goat cream cheese

½ small bowl cress,
leaves plucked and minced

**3 RED ONIONS**

# TARTE FLAMBÉE
## WITH GOAT CHEESE

Knead flour, canola oil, water, and ½ tsp salt into an
elastic dough. Let it rest,
covered, for 30 minutes. Wash
the apple, get rid of the core,
and cut into thin slices. Using a
pan filled with 1 tbsp olive oil,
fry briefly on each side, and then
put aside. Peel the onions, cut
into slices, and briefly sauté in
the rest of the olive oil.

Preheat the oven to 410°F (210°C), or
375°F (190°C) for a convection oven.
Roll the crust out thin on a floured
work surface, then place on a baking
sheet with parchment paper. Mix the goat
cream cheese with milk and chopped rosemary
and spread out on top of the tarte flam-
bée. Cover with apples and onions, and season with pepper. Crumble the goat cheese into
pieces and spread out over the top as well.
Bake for 20 minutes, until golden brown.
Before serving, sprinkle with cress.

**SERVES
2 TO 4**

29

½ package (200 g) Frozen Puffed Pastry, Thawed

3 SPRIGS OF THYME

5¼ oz (150 g) mountain cheese (Emmental, Gruyère, or Fontina)

SALT & PEPPER

CREAM: ⅔ CUP (150 ML)

MILK: ⅔ CUP (150 ML)

1 tbsp butter for the pan

18 oz (500 g) thick root vegetables, i.e...

3 cloves garlic

PARSNIP

CARROTS

RED BEETS

CELERIAC

GOLDEN BEETS

lentils for blind baking

# roasted root vegetable tart

Makes one 9.5 in (24 cm) tart

Preheat the oven to 300ºF (150ºC). Grease the tart pan and lay out the puffed pastry so that it stretches over the rim on every side. Stick a fork into the pastry at the bottom of the pan multiple times, to create small holes in the crust. Cut a piece of parchment paper big enough to completely cover the dough, and place it in the pan. Fill the pan up to the edge with lentils. Bake in the oven for about 40 minutes. Then take out the lentils and the paper, and bake the crust for about 5 more minutes until it is golden brown.

Heat cream and milk in a pot, and season with hearty pinches of salt and pepper. Peel the garlic and chop finely. Wash the thyme and remove the leaves. Put both of them in the cream mixture and let cook for about 5 minutes. Then, mix in the grated cheese and set aside.

Peel the vegetables and use a mandoline slicer to cut them into ⅛-inch (3-mm) thick slices. Place them on the crust in overlapping rows, and pour the cream sauce over the top. Bake for 50 more minutes in the oven. If the tart is getting too dark, cover with aluminum foil and let bake until the time is up.

GINGER TO TASTE

½ cup (120 ml) vegetable broth

1 green chili pepper

½ tsp ground cinnamon

1¼ cups (280 ml) coconut milk

½ tsp ground cumin

1 baby pineapple

LEMON JUICE TO TASTE

18 oz (500 g) saddle of pork steaks

½ tsp ground coriander

⅔ CUP (50 G) COCONUT CHIPS, TOASTED IN THE OVEN

½ tsp curry powder

⅓ LB (150 G) PEARL ONIONS

1 tbsp yellow curry paste

salt

½ tsp mild paprika

4 TBSP VEGETABLE OIL

# Indian Pineapple Curry

Take the pork steaks off of the rind and slice the meat into strips. Peel the pearl onions and cut each of them in half. Remove the rind and stalk of the pineapple, and then cut the flesh of the fruit into $1/3$-in (1-cm) wide pieces. Peel the ginger and grate finely. Clean the chili pepper and cut into rings, removing the seeds.

Heat 2 tbsp oil in a large pan or wok. Add the onions, chili pepper, and pineapple chunks, and sauté for 5 minutes, stirring frequently. Set aside on a plate. Then sear the meat in the rest of the oil for 5 minutes and set that aside as well. Afterward, add the curry paste, ginger, and spices to the pan and roast until the contents give off an aromatic smell. Deglaze with the vegetable broth, add the coconut milk and let the liquid come to a boil. Put all the set-aside ingredients in the pan again and let simmer for 2 more minutes. Season to taste with salt and lemon juice, and garnish with the coconut chips.

Tip: Serve with basmati rice

Serves 4

4 stems flat leaf parsley

1 2/3 cups (200 g) red Camargue rice

1 BELL PEPPER

2 TBSP SUNFLOWER OIL

2 TBSP WHITE BALSAMIC VINEGAR

1/2 TSP SPICY CURRY POWDER

1/2 TSP MILD PAPRIKA

1/2 tbsp tomato paste

1 Zucchini

1 TSP FINE SEA SALT

1/2 tsp ground coriander

1/2 tsp ground cumin

# Red Rice Salad

Serves **2**

Soak the rice for about 1 hour in water. Then pour water into a pan and let boil, seasoning with salt. Add the rice and cook for 30 minutes. In a colander, drain and rinse the rice, and then let dry.

Wash the parsley, pat dry, and chop coarsely. Clean the pepper and the zucchini and cut into ³/₄-in (2-cm) cubes. In a pan, heat the spices without oil, until they give off a pleasant aroma. Add the tomato paste and vegetables, sauté for 3 minutes, and deglaze with the vinegar.

Put the rice in a serving bowl, add vegetables and sunflower oil, and mix everything well. Season to taste with sea salt and sprinkle with parsley. Mix everything together well and serve cold.

1 1/4 cups (300 ml) vegetable oil for frying

OIL

1 head endive

1/2 cup (150 g) greek yogurt

2 tomatoes on the vine, cleaned and diced

1 bundle cilantro

1 ripe avocado, diced

4 large flour tortillas

1/2 TSP BAKING POWDER

1 TBSP GROUND CORIANDER

salt
pepper

2 tsp lime juice

1 1/2 CUPS (300 G) DRIED CHICKPEAS

1 BUNCH PARSLEY

Soak the chickpeas in a substantial amount of water overnight. The next day, drain the chickpeas and wash them. Puree together with coarsely chopped parsley and baking powder, and season with salt and coriander. Heat up oil to 340°F (170°C) in a saucepan. Make small balls out of the dough and deep fry them in hot oil. Remove from the oil and let dry.

Wash the salad, dry it, and cut it into small pieces. Season the yogurt with lime juice, salt, and pepper. Chop the cilantro coarsely. Separate the tortillas and cover them with lettuce, tomato, and avocado. Put 4 falafel on top of each. Drizzle with yogurt, sprinkle coriander over the top, and roll each wrap together tightly.

# Falafel

## Serves 4

mmm...
DELICIOUS

1 bunch mixed herbs

1 VEGETABLE SLICER

8–10 WOODEN SKEWERS

12–14 oz (350–400 g)

COD FILLET

3 WAXY LARGE POTATOES

3 TBSP CONCENTRATED BUTTER

juice from ½ lemon

⅓ CUP (75 ML) SAFFLOWER OIL

⅓ CUP (75 ML) OLIVE OIL

2 egg yolks

1 TSP MUSTARD

AND:
-SALT
-PEPPER

38

# FISH IN A POTATO CRUST

For the mustard dip, put the egg yolks and 2 tsp lemon juice in a tall container. Pour in the oil, and then use an immersion blender to mix, starting from the bottom of the container and gradually

Remove the skin from the cod fillet and slice into 1¼-in (3-cm) wide pieces. Season with salt, pepper, and the rest of the lemon juice.

Peel the potatoes and insert lengthwise into a vegetable slicer. Use the slicer to create long pieces of potato that resemble spaghetti. Put the pieces of fish on the skewers and wrap with the

**SERVES 2 TO 4**

getting higher while also gaining speed, until a homogeneous mass forms. Season to taste with salt and pepper. Rinse off the herbs, dry them, chop coarsely, and add them to the mixture. Puree finely once again.

potato spaghetti. Heat up the concentrated butter in a large pan, place the fish skewers carefully aside, and fry for about 5 minutes on every side. Let them drip dry, and serve with herb mayonnaise.

39

2 chicken breasts
(each about 7 oz [200 g])

salt + pepper

1 tbsp
olive oil

**2 cups (120 g)
Panko
breadcrumbs**

1 GREEN
CHILI PEPPER

1 SMALL
PIECE GINGER
(CA. ³/₄ IN
[2 CM])

²/₃ CUP
(80 G)
CANNING
SUGAR
2:1

2 eggs,
beaten

²/₃ cup
(80 g) flour

2 LIMES

4-6 STEMS
FRESH CILANTRO

1 cup
(¼ l)

VEGETABLE OIL

½
honeydew
melon
(ca. 14 oz [400 g])

40

1 shallot

# Chicken Nuggets

For the dip, get rid of the pit in the melon, and cut off the rind with a knife. Dice the fruit finely. Peel the ginger and chop it up. Put it in a pot with the diced melon and canning sugar, slowly bring to a boil, and then set aside. Peel the shallot and dice finely. Clean the chili pepper and cut into rings, taking out the seeds. Season with salt, pepper, and the juice from 1 lime. Pluck the leaves from the cilantro and chop them up. Stir them into the mixture. Cut the other lime into slices and place on top of the dip to serve.

Rinse the chicken breast, dab dry, and cut 1-cm thick strips lengthwise. Season on all sides with salt and pepper and dredge, first in flour, then in whisked egg, and lastly in Panko. Heat the oil in a pan. Fry the chicken nuggets on both sides for about 4 minutes, until golden brown. Let dry and serve together with the melon salsa.

# Ratatouille Paella

Heat 6 tbsp olive oil in a pan. Sear the eggplant first, then the zucchini, and finally the onion and tomato, on all sides. Set aside on a plate. Pluck the cherry tomatoes from the stem and rinse. Peel the garlic and chop finely.

Preheat the oven to 390°F (200°C), or 355°F (180°C) for a convection oven. Heat up the rest of the olive oil in a large pan, add garlic, shallots, and rice, and sauté until glassy. Deglaze with vegetable broth, and add the herbs and saffron threads. Let everything cook for 10 minutes and season heartily with salt and pepper. Then, layer the fried vegetables on the rice in overlapping rows. Place the cherry tomatoes on top. Season to taste once more and bake for 15 minutes in the oven.

TIP: EXTRA OLIVE OIL CAN ALSO BE DRIZZLED ON THE VEGETABLES UPON SERVING, AS DESIRED.

½ bunch basil

2 stems oregano

8 PICKLED GREEN PEPPERS

16 black olives

4 TBSP OLIVE OIL

1¾ OZ (50 G) SALAMI, CUT INTO SLICES

3 plum tomatoes

7 oz (200 g) spaghetti

2 garlic cloves

2 mozzarella spheres

4 eggs

# SPAGHETTI PIZZA

Cook spaghetti in salt water until it is al
dente, rinse with cold water, and put into
a bowl. Peel and press the garlic. Whisk
the eggs, and season with garlic, plucked
oregano leaves, salt, and pepper. Mix in
with the pasta.

Heat 2 tbsp olive oil in a pan (9 ⅖-in [24-cm]
in diameter). Take half of the pasta-egg mixture,
distribute it evenly throughout the pan, and cook
both sides until golden brown. Set on a baking
sheet, and then do the exact same thing with the
rest of the pasta.

Preheat the oven to 355°F (180°C), or with
a convection oven 320°F (160°C). Clean the
tomatoes and slice in thin rings. Then
cut those slices in half, and spread out
on the spaghetti pizzas. Cut the pickled
green peppers into rings and the mozzarella
into thin slices. Place the salami, olives,
pickled green peppers, and
mozzarella on the pizzas. Bake in
the oven for 12 minutes. Meanwhile,
rinse the basil, shake dry, and
pluck the leaves. Before serving,
sprinkle over the pizzas.

45

1 baby pineapple

RED GRAPES AS DESIRED, WITHOUT SEEDS

½ organic lemon

1 bunch peppermint

1 dragonfruit

2 MANDARIN ORANGES

1 NAVEL ORANGE

2 Kiwi

½ Galia melon

½ ripe papaya

1 RIPE MANGO

½ CUP (120 ML) WATER

2-3 PASSION FRUIT

48

AND: ½ cup (100 g) sugar

6 lychees

1 APPLE, I.E., GRANNY SMITH

1 SMALL BOWL STRAWBERRIES

# Fruit Salad

**Serves 4 to 5**

For the dressing, cut the passion fruit in half, remove the seeds with a spoon, and put into a small pot. Cut the lemons into slices, and mix in, along with the sugar and water. Let cook for 5 minutes, and take out the slices of lemon. Rinse the peppermint, shake dry, chop into small pieces, and add to the syrup. Puree everything finely and let cool.

Peel the orange and the mandarin oranges, and cut out each of the segments. Take the lychees out of the shell, cut in half, and take out the seeds. Peel the kiwis and cut them into slices. Wash the apple, core it, and cut into small pieces. Remove the seeds from the papaya, peel it, and dice it. Peel the mango, and cut the flesh of the fruit into small pieces. Remove the pineapple rind and core and cut it into bite-size pieces. Wash the grapes and cut them in half. Cut the passionfruit in half, squeeze it out of its shell, and cut it into small pieces. Remove the melon rind and dice. Clean the strawberries and cut them in half.

Fill a large bowl with all of the ingredients. Pour the dressing over the top, mix everything together, and keep cold for 1 hour.

7 oz (200 g) milk chocolate

7 oz (200 g) dark chocolate

1 cup (125 g) flour

3½ oz (100 g) white chocolate

2 eggs

⅔ cup + 3 tbsp (200 ml) cream

⅔ cup (125 g) sugar

½ cup (125 g) butter

1 baking pan 6 x 10 in (15 x 25 cm), lined with parchment paper

½ cup + 4 tsp (50 g) cacao

1 vanilla bean, pulp scraped out

50

# TRIPLE CHOCOLATE BROWNIES

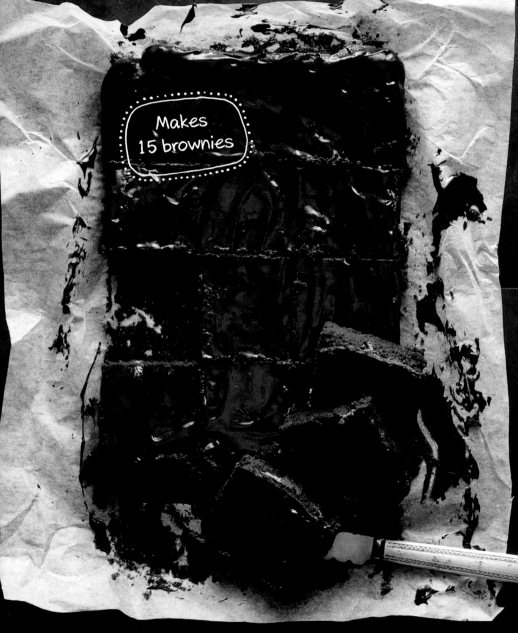

Makes 15 brownies

Preheat the oven to 390°F (200°C). Chop chocolate, separated by type, finely. Stir the eggs and the sugar together into a creamy mass. Mix with vanilla pulp, cacao, and ½ cup (125 ml) cream. Melt 4 ⅓ oz (125 g) dark chocolate with the butter using a double boiler, and then add it to the egg mixture. Mix in the flour a little at a time, as well as 4 ⅓ oz (125 g) milk chocolate, and then the white chocolate. Fill the pan with the dough and bake for 25 minutes.

For the icing, melt the rest of the chocolate and add the rest of the cream to it. Stir until creamy and spread on the cooled brownies.

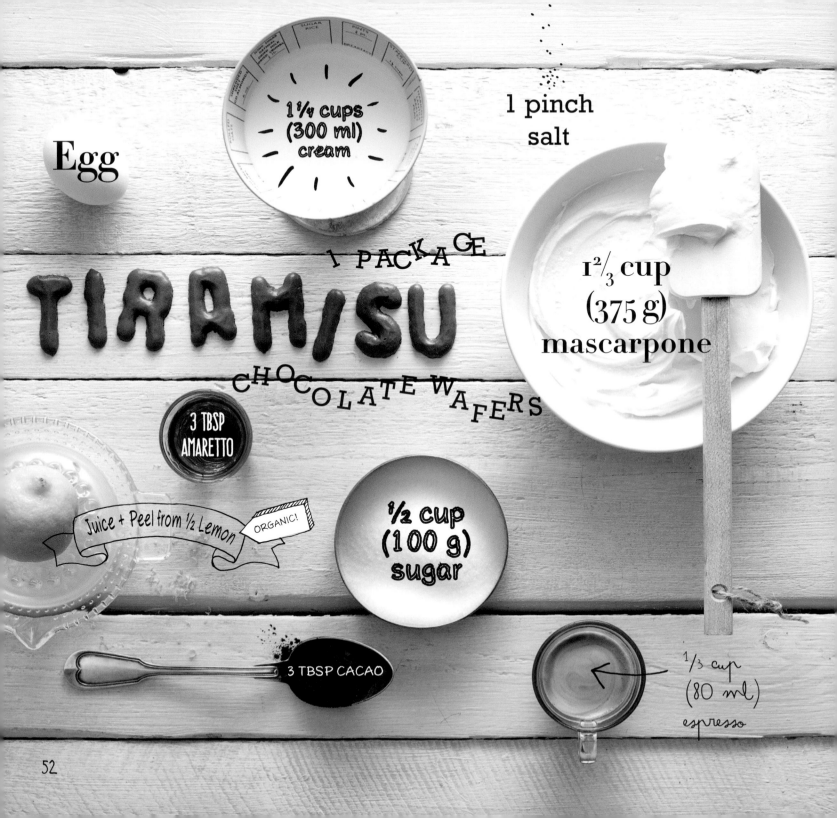

1¼ cups
(300 ml)
cream

1 pinch
salt

Egg

1 PACKAGE

TIRAMISU

1²⁄₃ cup
(375 g)
mascarpone

CHOCOLATE WAFERS

3 TBSP
AMARETTO

Juice + Peel from ½ Lemon   ORGANIC!

½ cup
(100 g)
sugar

3 TBSP CACAO

⅓ cup
(80 ml)
espresso

# tiramisu with Chocolate Wafers

Roughly chop up the chocolate wafers. Beat egg, sugar, salt, lemon zest, and lemon juice in the top of a double boiler until foamy. Then, let cool a little in cold water, while stirring. Mix in mascarpone, beat the cream until you have stiff peaks and fold in.

Spread out half of the gingersnaps at the bottom of a round baking dish. Mix amaretto and espresso and sprinkle half of it over the top. Then, put in half of the cream. Layer in the rest of the gingersnaps, and distribute the leftover liquids and half of the leftover cream over the top. Place the cream that is left into a decorating bag with a round tip and squeeze dots of icing onto the surface. Dust with cocoa powder, and preferably store somewhere cold for one day.

Serves 4

1 CUP + 2 TBSP (140 G) PISTACHIOS

12-cup muffin pan, 10 cups lined with parchment paper

1 ⅔ CUP (200 G) POWDERED SUGAR

¼ CUPS (300 G) SOFT BUTTER

1 ¾ cup (260 g) blackberries, plus 10 extra for garnishing

½ tsp cornstarch

¼ CUP (30 G) FLOUR

4 eggs, separated

1 pinch salt

1 TBSP WATER

# Blackberry Cupcakes

Makes 10

Preheat the oven to 340°F (170°C). Stir 3½ oz (100 g) of butter in with 2½ oz (70 g) of powdered sugar. Then mix the egg yolks in with that. Beat the egg whites with the salt until stiff, and then gradually add in the 2½ oz (70 g) powdered sugar. Blend the beaten egg whites, flour, and finely chopped pistachios into the butter mixture. Distribute the dough into the cups, and bake for 25 minutes. Boil down the blackberries in a pot. Mix cornstarch and water and then add them in. Strain everything and let cool. Beat the rest of the butter and the leftover powdered sugar until foamy, and stir in the blackberry sauce. Pipe the icing onto the cupcakes and garnish with blackberries.

25 butter cookies

12²⁄₃ OZ (350 G) DARK CHOCOLATE

1¼ cups (300 ml) cream

²⁄₃ CUP (150 G) ROOM-TEMPERATURE BUTTER

2 TBSP INSTANT COFFEE POWDER

2 TBSP COCOA POWDER

# CHOCOLATE ICE BOX CAKE

For 1 loaf pan

Chop the chocolate into small pieces. Bring the cream to a boil in a pot and take it off the stove. Dissolve instant coffee powder in the hot cream. Add butter, cocoa powder, and chocolate, and let the ingredients melt while stirring.

Cover the pan with parchment paper or aluminum foil, and spread approx. 3 heaping tbsp of the chocolate mass onto the bottom of the pan. Then place the first layer of cookies on top. Place 3 more tbsp chocolate cream on the cookies and continue this pattern, until all the chocolate or all the cookies have been used up. Cover, and keep in the refrigerator for at least 8 hours.

Tip: Before serving the ice box cake, sprinkle with cocoa powder.

57

3 1/2 oz (100 g) amaretto cookies

4 ripe peaches

2 TBSP COARSE SUGAR

2 1/2 CUPS (300 G) FLOUR

3/4 cup (60 g) oatmeal

2 tbsp sugar

2/3 CUP (80 G) CANNING SUGAR 1:3

1 egg yolk

1/2 lemon

1 vanilla pod

1 cup (230 g) butter

1/4 cup + 3 tbsp (100 ml) ice cold water

1 TSP SALT

2 stems basil

# Peach Tart in Short Crust Pastry

Mix flour, oatmeal, sugar, and salt. Cut the butter into small pieces, add it in, and mix until crumbly. Then, with the cold water, quickly work into a dough. Keep cold for 1 hour.

In the meantime, wash the peaches, pit them and cut them into 8 slices. Cut the vanilla pod in half and scrape out the beans. Mix the vanilla beans with canning sugar and the peaches. Press the lemon and add the juice. Put the cookies in a freezer bag and crush them. Pluck the basil leaves from the stems, chop them, and add to the peaches along with the cookies.

Preheat the oven to 350°F (175°C). Roll out the short crust pastry into a circle (approx. 12 inches [30 cm] in diameter). Place the peach mixture in the middle, leaving a 2⅓ in (6 cm) wide crust around the edge. Fold the dough over on 5 sides and press down lightly. Whisk the egg yolk with 1 tbsp water and brush the dough with that mixture. Sprinkle the coarse sugar on top and bake the galette in the oven for about 35 minutes, until golden brown.

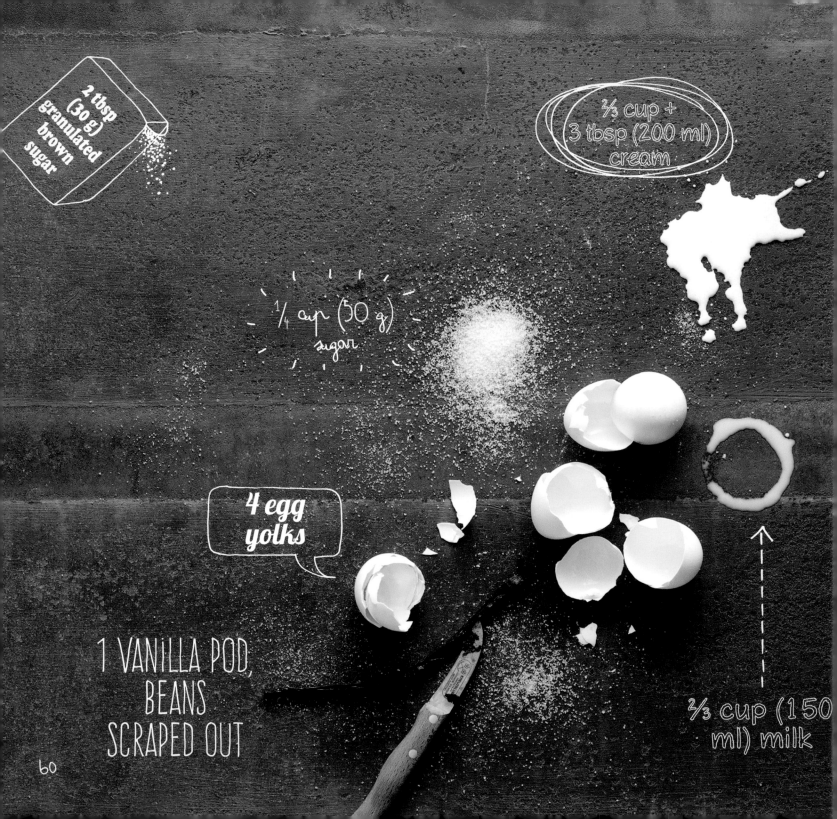

# crème brûlée

Preheat the oven to 285°F (140°C), or for a convection oven 250°F (120°C). Bring the milk, cream, and vanilla beans to a boil in a pot. Beat the egg yolk and confectioner's sugar in a bowl until foamy. Stir continuously, and slowly pour in the hot vanilla cream. Pour the mixture immediately through a colander and into a different bowl. Then, distribute into 4 oven-safe glass bowls (each 6 oz [175 ml], or 5 smaller bowls). Place in a flat baking dish and fill with enough hot water to cover ⅔ of the bowls.

Leave the baking dish in the oven for 1 hour. In the meantime, let the cream cool fully, preferably overnight. Before serving, sprinkle evenly with the brown granulated sugar. Caramelize with a Bunsen burner, until a light brown crust forms.

Serves
**4 to 5**

61

3 ½ OZ (100 G)
MANGO

**3½ oz (100 g)
yogurt**

3 ½ oz (100 g) fresh raspberries
(alternatively frozen berries)

1 RIPE BANANA

# Banana · Raspberry
## MANGO SMOOTHIE

Tip: If the smoothie is too thick, simply add a splash of water.

Serves 2

Fill a blender with the yogurt. Peel the banana, coarsely chop it, and add it in. Place the raspberries in a colander, briefly plunge into cold water, and carefully dab dry. Also throw into the blender.

Peel the mango, cut the fruit into cubes, and add that in as well. Mix everything together until smooth and serve in glasses.

Skyhorse Publishing books
may be purchased
in bulk at special
discounts for sales
promotion, corporate
gifts, fund-raising, or
educational purposes.
Special editions can
also be created                to
specifications. For                details,
contact the                Special Sales
Department,                Skyhorse
Publishing,                307 West 36th
Street,                11th Floor, New York,
NY                10018 or
info@        skyhorsepublishing.com.

Cover photo credit: Oliver
Brachat

Print ISBN: 978-1-63220-672-5
Ebook ISBN: 978-1-63220-906-1

Printed in China

Skyhorse® and Skyhorse
Publishing® are
registered trademarks
of Skyhorse Publishing,
Inc.®, a Delaware
corporation.

Visit our website at
http://www.skyhorsepublishing.com.

10 9 8 7 6 5 4 3 2 1

Library of Congress
Cataloging-in-
Publication Data
is available on file.

64